EARLY WINTER

EARLY WINTER

Learning to live, love
and laugh again
after a painful loss

HOWARD BRONSON

A BESTSELL BOOK
6 Samba Circle
Sandwich, MA 02563

Permission should be addressed in writing to: Bestsell
Publications, 6 Samba Circle, Sandwich, MA 02563

Library of Congress Cataloging-in-Publication Data

Bronson, Howard F., 1953-
    Early winter.
    1. Consolation. 2. Bronson, Howard F., 1953-
3. Bronson, Gordon. I. Title.
BV4905.2.B697   1987   155.9'37   87-13142
ISBN 0-9616807-2-5

Printed in the United States of America.

And with deepest thanks to Irma, Rebecca and
Lisa Bronson who edited my creation with a fine
balance of ruthlessness and delicacy.

HB

Dedication

LisaLove

if i didn't have you

kissing my iron-coated heart
til the brokenness showed through;
stumbling through that cold, dark cave
would have been such a lonely crawl.

When it hurts so new,
I think of you
and the babies too.

CONTENTS

Cherished Grief

My love, my lover, my other self, my best friend
has died.

He is gone from me. I am alone.

No matter that I am surrounded by friends
and relatives
and children
and everyone—

I am so alone.

The longing for him and the missing of him
is an acute physical ache.

The loneliness and the quiet is anguish.

Time and I are engaged in battle—
Time wants to assuage my pain
but I will not cooperate.
I will keep my pain as a pearl.
I will spin a shell around my anguish
and hide it deep within my heart
So no one else may see it.

Now I can come back into my life
and be who I am amongst the living.
And I will be a person who will converse,
play bridge, take classes, tell stories and some-
*　　　times smile.*

I may even love someone. sometime. somewhere.

but I will always treasure this dark jewel
and keep my sorrow hidden evermore.

This is what I had felt. Put it away—don't burden everyone with your sorrow. Get on with your life. But now my son has opened our hearts and re-examined this hidden pearl from many dimensions.

With great pride I invite you to enjoy with me this collection of poignant essays and vignettes.

Irma Bronson

Introduction

I am your parent
> *child*
> *spouse*
> *sibling*
> *or friend.*

I am gone, forever gone.

I am not coming back.

I will always know that you loved me.

You will always know that I loved you.

Someone you love very dearly has died and the pain, sadness and confusion seem too great for any words to mean anything. Even life itself can feel hollow and meaningless. Yet, at the same time, life continues.

This is a book about the newness of life and the inherent changes that we must learn to live with. That newness is a gift from our past loved ones.

Death always seems to happen too soon. Be it the robust man struck down in the prime of life or the ailing patient who could have held on just a bit longer, creature death makes its rude arrival a moment, a year, a lifetime before we expect it.

My dad's unexpected death left me longing for a companion to help me come to terms with the many complex issues of dealing with the death of someone who was never ever supposed to die.

Shortly after his death, I found myself displaying unusual outward strength, while an internal loneliness began erupting uncomfortably inside of me. Where was that magic companion? No matter how many people loved or hugged me, I was incredibly isolated.

Two things kept me going during this period. One was an inherent sense of duty to make my father proud. The other was the grandchildren he will never know. I promised myself that they would know him.

After a week or two of traditional mourning, I kept my pain dormant simply because death is something part of this world doesn't want to know about. The only real way to become remotely acquainted with this creature death is to lose someone you really love.

With his passing, I found myself a member of a society whose membership was exclusive to those who have lost a special loved-one; that sharing of an immediate common bond and that same inexplicable feeling of not just loss, but of being lost. Worst of all, the person you want to talk to about it with, the person who can ameliorate your suffering, is gone forever.

It is to my lost comrades that I write so we may all share the struggle of surviving a great loss and the building of a new hope and spirit that for the first time, is all our own.

My struggle has been to breathe new life into my words and my writing has become an accounting of an inner awakening that I never imagined experiencing as a young man. Death does more than hurt for a little while, so I set out to learn how to live with it.

Our culture does everything possible to avoid or forget pain. But to forget the pain of a lost loved-one is to forget their love as well. I can still clearly remember his commanding voice, that smile and laugh that warmed a room. And so much more; the great life and power of this man, all reduced to a memory in just one instant.

Thank God for memories. These are what I share in the hope they will help you keep your memories strong as you nurture your new life and explore the long road of saying goodbye to that special person who touched your life.

Though your struggle is personal only to you, there are millions of people struggling with issues they must face about a lost loved-one. And the issues must be faced.

Through these writings, you may find that you are not alone and that you can put your life in solid order as you discover that the special warmth and wisdom of your loved-one gets stronger with time.

Come share my tears, my anger and my laughter. You'll learn that you can feel better, resolve the struggles, and feel good about developing a whole new life. Find companionship in these writings and make them your own. And in time your new inner strength will be your best companion.

Yes . . .
these are words and
in pain of loss
words ring as empty noise.
Time and love nurture painful growth
and whisper life-change.

1

THE DAY AFTER

A New Lifetime

"I used to talk to him." I woke up again with the cold itch of tears dragging across my face like icy chains. "I used to talk to him." It was 3 a.m.

Late last night, about six hours after he died, I thought I would be okay. I hadn't cried in years. But this night, I cried, I let it all out hoping the hurt would begin to abate. So infantile was my knowledge of death.

Where did that laugh come from! I heard it clearly. It was his laugh. That hearty, husky chortle that made you feel warm, accepted, comfortable. But he was dead. Where did that laugh come from?

I hear the echo of his laughter as he and my mother joked together. I can feel his joy.

The power of that laughter, never to be heard again.

His death made me fear that my last best friend was gone forever. He was the one with whom I would spend those hours sharing my greatest hopes, my most desperate doubts. He gave why's and he gave wisely.

My best friend is forever gone. I'm alone now.

I panic as the realization of this void churns through my heart. This is pure sadness, an emptiness like I have never known. Tears flow rudely against my cheeks. My pillow is too wet to sleep on.

If my father saw this display, he'd be so disappointed. The children of this man were not to cry. But I feel pain this day. What do I do dad? Only you could answer these questions so I would believe them.

There is no sobbing, just tears, no noise to wake up my wife. She looks beautiful, so peaceful. "You take care of her," dad would say. "She is your most precious asset." But I still can't share all this grief with anybody. The marriage is fine, but the love is still young.

This quandary is between my father and me.

Was I wrong to make my father my best friend, my hero, my teacher? Should I have ever risked having a best friend? At this moment, the pain of the loss is the only thing greater than the joy of that friendship.

Nothing will ever replace that intimacy. That's my agony, life's first real pain. This new creature that has taken up permanent residence in my soul.

So what keeps me going? His wish? He wuddawantedit that way? I'm a man. I'm strong. I'm tough. I can feel this burdensome sense of added responsiblity to help pull the family through this horror.

"He wuddawantedit that way." That's a great stock phrase but it makes no sense whatsoever. He can't tell us how to deal with his own death. It just isn't that simple.

It's the suffering of others that keeps me going right now. The need to do anything to help alleviate suffering, not add to it. My sorrow is nothing compared to what I see my mother going through. I tell her so. "We had a good life," she would say. "We had thirty-five wonderful years together."

She must have said that a hundred times today. I have needed to keep making her say that to assure myself that she was coming along okay. But she wasn't. She knew I needed to hear that. He was too grand, too much alive for any philosophy to serve this strange new situation.

These are the most painful and strange days as we struggle to believe the unbelievable and to realize that we are still alive.

No one can even begin to comprehend this dizzying horror until they lose someone they really love. We all know we can make a future but on this early winter day, there is only pain and despair.

I'm bleeding from my father's heart,
a candle crying
dark red droplets
falling from a cruel fire.

My father's heart.

waxen tears leak pain
droplets glisten years

No one hears.
No one speaks.

Tears wax abundant
harden lifeless

I bleed coldly.

2

THE MOMENTS OF KNOWING

The Shower of Tears

"I'm sure he'll be fine," my wife kept saying calmly. "He's never been sick in his life."

There were no tears yet. We were just in the car speeding to the L.A. airport. My father-in-law had called to say that my dad was in the emergency room at the hospital. They were trying to get his signs to stabilize and it didn't look good.

"Lisa, I'm sure he's dead."

"You don't know that. You have to think positively," she responded.

But I knew something was very wrong, even without knowing the details. When we arrived at the airport, we just left the car at some hotel and bought tickets. Then came the time to call home again.

I had no positive feelings as I usually do. Dad was always in perfect health so if he were struggling in an emergency room, I just knew something was very wrong. I was as prepared for this as anyone could be.

My father-in-law answered on the first ring. He immediately put mother on. I knew she would be very sensitive about whatever the news was. She has an excellent speaking manner. I knew she would make the news more palatable.

"Howard," her voice was firm, "Daddy's dead."

I was as shocked by her directness as I was by the news. I acted very calm and supportive on the phone and told her we would be landing in Boston in five hours. Then I hung up and Lisa and I cried in each other's arms, glued together. This was that painful moment of knowing the thing we never wanted to know. The tears began and I had no idea how to stop them. I only knew we had a plane to catch in a few minutes.

As we walked from the phone, my first steps were so peculiar, baby steps, the first I would have to take alone.

I learned that I could still cry and that I couldn't stop it but there was almost no place we could cry that first week. People were always there and the Bronsons were not a crying family. Well, the women could cry a little but the men, not allowed.

I always envied women who could cry when necessary. It seemed like such a healthy way of expressing sadness. But men fear crying as a sign of weakness. So the men cry in the shower. The tears kind of get lost in the water and no one has to know.

When I cried, I couldn't think. Normally, thoughts were like shooting stars racing everywhere. The tears were my psychological coffee-break.

I hadn't cried in years. Nothing hurt that much. Not a broken relationship, business losses, illness. There were some depressing times but that's very different from real sadness.

Depression is something I could always recover from. It was just a natural part of living. Death was so definite. No turning back.

For weeks, I would sneak my tears in the shower, then in the car on the way to work. Finally one day, they just stopped and I buried myself in my work for months. I struggled to fill this shower of emptiness.

Thereafter, I would experience a tinge of longing or an odd shock as if I had just heard the news. These were momentary waves of horror that still hit me occasionally.

I really loved my dad.

If There's Anything, Anything
I Can Do, Just Let Me Know

The week after. The shock. The horror. The people. The many couples and families still safe and intact as we sat fragmented but somehow temporarily comfortable in this artificial frenzy.

For six days after his death, it was one continuous gathering of all our friends and relatives. We were never a family to display much negative emotion in public so this time of friends was very helpful because with all the people to talk to, there was really no time to grieve. In fact, we found ourselves consoling our friends rather than the other way around.

As I look back on this period, I think we were all still in shock and just needed to put that awful moment of death as far behind us as possible. Just get us through this first week and we'll all be okay.

Our friends numbed the pain and helped ease the shock but no one could make sense of it. I really saw the courage of people when they showed up at a time like this. It was difficult to even be there. All these people, scared, sad and awkward, but there. Mom and dad had made some wonderful friends.

It seemed that the real friends were there, and that's all that was needed. They were sad with us. They were lost with us. They were there.

The Amazing Exploding Family

Right after my dad had been declared dead, everyone seemed in control but nobody was. One moment we all seemed fine and the next moment we were devastated. The pilot was gone and none of us really knew how to fly the plane.

I kept thinking of us as the amazing exploding family. We were all over the place, trying to draw upon any strength, any platitude, any philosophy just to get us through this crazy dream.

It was all so useless, waiting for him to come back. Or just waiting for so much time to go by, that the pain would finally lessen, as pain often does with time.

In one sense, life was now so harshly real and in another, all practical aspects of life seemed to fade away. Though I can't speak for my siblings or mother, I suspect we all wanted to grab some control of that metaphorical airplane, before it crashed.

To this end, I felt eminently more responsible and connected to a family I hadn't seen much of over the five years prior, with the exception of bi-weekly phone-calls to my dad. As soon as I could wrap up my business commitments in L.A., my wife and I relocated to Boston to become part of the family again. I felt a much greater sense of obligation to my siblings and mother.

For the first six months after his death, I did nothing but work. Then I slowed down the struggle to become the master writer/marketeer. No one to share it all with. I felt lost without this brilliant mind to love and advise me. There was no one to impress anymore but the responsibilities of life had progressed to the point where I couldn't turn and run.

So I floated between fact and fantasy—wanting children but still acting like a child. I required almost a year before I began building my business back up as I developed a new thirst for success.

No question about it, when a loved-one dies, your life explodes. It's a time to find your courage. It's a time to draw upon the wisdom and spirit of that loved-one to put the fragments back together.

Eventually when all the dust settles, you will give your departed friend cause to look down,

and smile.

A Change of Face

A few weeks after the funeral, my wife, younger sister and I grabbed a football and just escaped to a park somewhere. We were trying to see if it was time for fun to rear its head. We threw the football a little, walked and my sister took some pictures.

I didn't see those pictures until about a year later. I could not believe my eyes. Normally, you look at a picture for a moment and that's it. I couldn't take my eyes off two of my sister and me. These were not just sad nor tired faces, they were old, burdened. I almost didn't recognize us. Yet we were young. It was as if we were wearing masks of our much older selves.

Mother spoke of a great weight over her heart, that she struggled to carry with her wherever she went. We understood. We could feel that weight.

We saw no promise of recovering from this odd malady. Some of my closest friends had told me they could read the pain in my face for several months.

Then after some time, this weight subsided and we began to feel and look younger again.

We even photographed younger.

Now unless they invented a new kind of camera that adds youth, I believe my observation is correct. The only thing I'm unsure of is whether the weight on our hearts has subsided or if we just got used to carrying it around.

When Daddy Died

a life we cried

A Life we cried.
Then We died.

A life we thought
to last so long,
last so long.

What went wrong?

Our new life starts,

with broken hearts,
we never planned,
one not so grand.

With broken hearts
when daddy died.

A life our own.
What Went Wrong?

"He Had A Good Life"

The year was 1965. We were at Haystack Ski Area in Wilmington, Vermont. With the wind-chill factor, the average temperature that day dipped to 28 degrees below zero Farenheit. Occasionally, the wind would die down and things would immediately warm up to a scorching minus 15 to 20 degrees. These were the kind of days that convinced most people that the end of the world was at hand.

On this blustery February morning, most New Englanders were indoors shivering as the mercury disappeared to the very base of their outdoor thermometers.

Mom was clever. She won some kind of executive privilege and got to stay in with the sane folks. My siblings and I were not so lucky and somehow found ourselves with skis on, bundled up and heading to chairlift one.

Led by my dad, we marched along, taking care not to breathe too much because it hurt our lungs. Dad was in his traditional ski outfit—just a sweater and a windbreaker.

"Look, no liftlines," he said as we scurried to the lift. I kept wondering what kind of crazy

34

people would keep the ski lift open on this day that the sun died.

Dad rode with Rebecca who was only eight at the time, Phyllis and Noah rode together and I went up alone. As I boarded the chair, I began counting down the seconds we had left before we could go inside with the sane people.

But now we were the rugged lot. As the chair deposited us at the top of the trail, dad kept saying, "Think warm." I was wishing warm. As we struggled a few feet down the hill, a gust of wind occasionally caught Rebecca and seemed to scoop her back to the top of the hill. Dad would rescue her and tell her to think warm. She'd look up to him with her big brown eyes and say, "We're having fun, aren't we?"

A little ways more down and dad would stop us all and say, "Look at that view!" Now I'm sure the view was beautiful but my eyelids were almost frozen together and even if I could see, visibility was only about two feet.

Well, eventually, we made it. I stopped counting down the seconds and finally found myself sitting in front of the fireplace waiting to see what would thaw.

We experienced a lot of these tests as we grew up. It's always a good laugh when the family gets together and recalls yet another one of these expeditions. As we were actually going through these experiences, they didn't seem quite as funny. We didn't realize we were being tested and conditioned for this crazy world.

My dad's life spanned 60 years and six months. He saw the beginning of flight and financial depressions. He fought in World War II and Korea. He made millions by being an honest, aggressive businessman and he saw it all get snatched away. He recovered and bounced back stronger than ever.

He was a results-getting leader and a loving family man. He demanded the best from his children, he forgave us for failing and praised us for trying and never giving up.

At his grave, a bronze plaque reads . . . "A Heart of Wisdom." His was a life of achievement and optimism in the face of hopelessness and despair. He found extra strength where most men gave up, took risks where other men elected to be safe.

The most important thing he taught me was about time. How long we live isn't nearly as important as how we live. Gordon really did have a good and full life and he worked and fought hard for it.

His untimely death robbed him of those years to sit and reflect back. Then again he was never one to sit and look back. He was always looking at the beauty of today and tomorrow, even in the face of blinding Arctic winds.

3

THE SUNNY PLACES

Dad's Youth Formula

If anyone really wanted to collapse the American economy once and for all, that person would take away our cherished personal belief that youth can last forever. We think, "Other people grow old and fade. Me, I'm gonna stay young." More than anything else, we spend billions based on the singular illusion that we can escape the clutches of Father Time forever or for at least a very long time.

Escape is the buzz word here. The rich and even the not-so-rich escape winter weather by flying to the sunny places. We escape problem marriages or other relationships by dissolving them. We escape bad health by staying away from unhealthy things.

The most important illusion is our escape from death itself. Our grey-haired or balding friends suddenly have their youthful locks again. Grandmothers are looking less like the mothers of their children and more like sisters.

My father was constantly described as a youthful man. I always heard his friends remark how young he looked. When he died, his friends mourned him as if he were a young man cut down in the prime of his life.

He was young. He was forever young yet he subscribed to none of the escape formulas to earn his eternal youth. We always felt so much in the center of life when we were around him and time moved so painlessly.

The strain of time and life confronted him often. He never sought to escape. By plunging into the challenges and learning to cope, he brought out the best in himself at any age and he knew real strength would reign supreme over the illusion of chasing youth.

Are we getting young again, are we better looking? It appears that while we're chasing youth in the wrong places, time is chipping away at our true youth. More than ever, we look at each other as either young or old and forego all of the more vital aspects of being human.

There's a faint voice inside many of us whispering, "Face yourself with all your foibles. Don't run from it. And the essence of life will be yours."

My dad never discussed anything like looking for that magical fountain of youth. He just lived his life with courage and the essence of life found him. He taught me that to remain young and vital, I had to face those things that I previously thought would make me old.

He is . . .
forever young

Perhaps one day
I will be older than he was

while still embracing the memory of my father

as a young man.

4

Fragile
Contract

Fragile Contract

My dad was like your dad. You know—immortal.

It's easy to write wills. Everyone understands about organizing the business end of dying, all those things the lawyers and accountants do to give the survivors security.

I must be unusual because I found little security from our lawyers or accountants or anybody for that matter. What I did experience was a deep sense of betrayal that no lawyer could rectify. I based much of my security on the implicit knowledge that dad would have a good long life. If he ever did die, it would take something extraordinarily tough to kill him.

This was my contract with the gods. This was life—cozy, secure, solid. When he died, when the gods breached this sacred contract, we were immediately confronted with the fragility of life. You really could "go just like that," as the expression goes.

Wow gods, you mean any of us could die that way just as easily, next week or tomorrow! For the first several fragile contract-less months, we were so protective of each other. Doctors' visits were traumatic. Talk of even minor surgery for any of us was forbidden. No one said so. We just all knew. After all, he entered the hospital in perfect health for a knee operation. A knee operation!

Ten days later he was dead.

That's enough to make you wonder if your next heart-beat is coming. Life is so fragile during this period. As tough as you might try to be, your resistance is much lower. Every virus finds you. In extreme cases, survivors can't find any reason to continue after a life-long companion dies so death finds a home for them as well.

Over a year after he died, my first child was born. I was struck by an awful conflict. What if I love this little one with all my heart and she dies too? Could I survive the risk? Luckily, with enough time and some reason, love won hands down.

It was a vulnerable time when advice was badly needed but so hard to ask for. You just have to get through that first year and love your babies. Mine are counting on me to be around forever.

The Worry's Gone

Humans are worriers. We worry about every-thing. Sex, death, money, self-image. Oh, we know it's bad to worry and of course we worry about that. Even the most mellow people you've ever known who don't seem to have a care in their heads; they worry that they have no worries.

And you and I, the smart ones, we know it's bad to worry. Just as we plug up one, another disturbing thought jumps right in to torment us.

When we're little, we worry. What would happen to us if Mommy or Daddy went away, not just in divorce, but forever? The thought is so scary, we can't even believe the thought exists.

So Mommy and Daddy give us great big hugs and promise to never go away. Usually that's true.

We grow up and the worry grows up. As a young man, I looked at my parents and noticed that they weren't young anymore but they were quite healthy and strong. I still worried and understood that worry, love and interdependence were all kind of intertwined.

You know by now that my dad was my lifeline of strength and confidence. He was incredibly strong in body and character, far too strong to just die from some illness.

If he ever died, it would have to be from an accident, like a plane crash or from a terrorist bullet while planning a new building in some third world country. And he rode those jet planes with unbounded trust and confidence.

I worried for his safety but knew that he loved the adventure of going out and getting new business. Always in great health, as long as one of those jets didn't crash, I was sure he'd live forever.

So when this healthy, robust man died so unexpectedly after a relatively minor knee operation, I was more than shocked and hurt; I was amazed.

This great, strong man was gone. A loved one's unexpected death hurts forever but something very interesting also happens. That major region of your body, mind and soul you had reserved for worry about that person, is now vacant.

The worry's gone but look what it took to get rid of it.

Shockland

nigh-nite, my babies.

Dream of toys . . .
and cookies and
dancing teddy bears.

pure-secure.

Sleeping smile.

Goodnight father.

"You'll be fine."

Off to sleep.

off to sleep

Siren blaring in the rain,
the last sounds heard.

No toys. No cookies.

no final dreams . . . .

Looking for Father

Right after dad died, none of us really went through a denial phase. It was more like a disbelief period. Would we never hear him laugh again, never see the excitement in his eyes as we greeted him, never hear his wisdom?

In an unbelievable instant, it's all gone. The automatic reaction for most is to be overwhelmed with a seemingly endless pain. Your body drags your aimless soul. You shuffle along, nowhere to escape the anguish until lo and behold, you bump into a loved-one or a family member. All the billions of people in the world and somehow, you meet one of the few people whose hug or voice can make a little difference.

Closely-knit family members cry as one. Relatives who never really got along suddenly love each other. Brothers put aside a lifetime of rivalry and suppressed emotion. They hug each other as if their relationship was the deepest in the world. It's a father's utopia. Alas, he won't see the love he always envisioned.

Lots of talk. Searching tearful eyes, lost. Looking for reasons. Confused, afraid. Looking for father.

Friends look at us. One says to me, "You could be another Gordon." Another tells my younger sister that she was his favorite. One of us laughs and it sounds a bit like his laugh. My brother rededicates his business aims. My mom works to take a firm grasp to become mother and father to grown children. We all watch each other for these hints of dad that come through. We listen, we hug. We look for father.

We were climbing out of a ravine, holding hands. The highest person could be no higher than the lowest sliding down. Hold tight, don't let go. There's no leader here, no wisdom that works. Time may heal but we hurt now. We climb a little, slip a little, find strength for each other and ourselves, then we take long rests.

Each of us appeared to be amplifying little traits that looked like his. At first it was comforting to trigger refreshing memories. After some time, it became annoying imitation and we gradually became ourselves again.

Nowadays I love the imitators. I see them everywhere. They remind all of us that no one will ever be him and no one will ever take the special place he held. The imitators remind me of how strong the original was. They keep his memory solid and very much alive. He was a great teacher and we have been inspired to learn

51

from him forever. We all work not to imitate the man but to honor what he stood for.

We observe, honor and wonder as we climb out of the ravine as ourselves.

The Stereo War

For the moment, the mighty gunships had ceased their thunderous fire and we could enter. I was thinking about the Beatles and all the changes that were happening in the U.S. as the sun baked our sweat-drenched bodies. We crept forward. When would the mortars rip through the icy silence?

Without warning, the guns again ring out their cruel death-knell. We tuck ourselves down low and pray for it to end.

It sounds like Vietnam but actually it was our living room in Newton, Massachusetts and the barrage of explosions emanated from our old hi-fi. During the sixties on some weekends, dad would gather up the entire multi-record set (although we swore it was all the same record) of *Victory At Sea* and stack 'em up on the stereo and the house became an audio war-zone for hours on end.

As a result, not one door-to-door salesman

ever called on us for fear of being blown to pieces.

"Hey dad," we'd beg, "wanna put on some music or somethin'?"

But *Victory At Sea* was music for him. These were the songs of the battles of World War II, the songs that he believed in because defending the freedom that we take for granted today meant so much to him.

Though he was an only child of proud and protective parents he believed that the freedom of his country was so important that he convinced his parents to let him join the Marines at age 17. He rose through the ranks quickly as he battled the Japanese throughout the South Pacific.

Death could have snapped him up at any moment and he did see many friends succumb to its cold embrace. When the war was over, his welcome home must have been the greatest joy of his parents' lives.

Under the G.I. bill, he attended Princeton and Yale and then began a thriving home-building company. That was cut short when he was called back to the Marines during the Korean conflict.

If his country needed him, he was ready. So when the Vietnam War came around, he was prepared to make the sacrifice of his life. If called upon, his sons would go to war.

My brother was approaching draft age. There were many nights I lay awake in fear that Noah would receive that telegram and I would never see him again.

No one said anything at first but something didn't seem right about this war. Dad's initial reaction was that the kids of the sixties had become spoiled and unappreciative. The conflicts between my brother and father became frightening. The stereo would be literally "blasting" in the background as my dad ostensibly commanded Noah in the ways of duty to one's country.

Noah fought back hard. No one was going to tell him to die for his country. Made sense to me as I hid in my room and waited for it all to end.

Things got uglier but not nearly as ugly as Vietnam. Dad grew to see that this was a war that was doing little more than killing children.

The tumultuous sixties spelled so many changes. Nothing seemed to be going right. Was this the proud country he had once fought for?

For a while the stereo went silent and ultimately, dad proved to be far more intelligent than stubborn. My brother and he made peace and by luck, my brother was not drafted. And my father even wrote a letter supporting the moral arguments of a neighbor who was a conscientious objector.

Even in my short life, I have seen the country's mood swing from Cold War to Hot Liberalism, from Castro and back to Rambo. I want reason to prevail but I understand that freedom is earned and must be protected. My freedom's a gift and I appreciate what my dad stood for.

He had said that all of the life he had after World War II was a gift. Bonus time. Perhaps an even greater gift was that he could see America slowly trying to learn from her mistakes as she blasted out that rocky path towards newer freedoms, and he didn't have to see his children die before he did.

I know he died as a strong and optimistic man, like a good soldier. I'll always appreciate that he taught me what to fight for.

But I'll pick my own record albums, thank you.

5

MOM'S DATING

Accepting No Substitutes

"How do you feel about your mom dating?" I've heard that question more than any other in the past few years, as if that's supposed to be the biggest thing on our minds—that mom find some sort of replacement and then we will all live happily ever after.

My standard answer is that it is none of my business. I just want her to be as happy and secure as possible. Do I evaluate the people she dates, like a worried parent? Of course not. I trust her judgement.

Do I compare the men mom has dated to my dad? How could I? But she has and her standards are incredibly high.

Oh, I will admit that sometimes I wished she would just marry one of these nice men. After all, I heard that these types of prospects were hard to come by at her age and I didn't want her to be alone. And I suppose I didn't want to worry about her as much.

Then I began seeing the pattern. She had a very good life with Gordon, exciting, adventurous, fun. A new marriage would have to offer more than security. She was already secure and very satisfied. She had had a dynamic relationship—a banquet. Even the best men after that could seem like ham sandwiches.

So as of this writing, her search continues but it's not even fair to call it a search. She is quite complete and maybe, as she says, one day she'll meet someone who will again lend a new excitement to her life.

It's not that she's living in the memory of a lost love but she is living to honor the people she loves.

Good luck, mom. Don't stay out too late.

6

SIBLING RIVALRY

Inward and Outward

What my parents hated most actually stemmed from what we did to try to please them the most. That is; to kill each other so the victor would win the greatest parental favor.

We were raised to win, or I should say, we were prepared to win. It all seemed innocent enough in the beginning. The Sunday football games (tackle) with my older brother and usually my dad, unless he was working. We used to have some great games in that long front field of our big old house.

Then one day as my popular and talented brother entered Junior High School, he didn't seem to have any time for it all anymore. It really hurt that my buddy didn't have time for me. It never occurred to me that things would change, that girls and all those other interests would take over his life. I just figured he'd always be there with me and for me.

So we grew apart, slowly and sadly as brothers often do. As we struggled to be the best and become the natural leaders we were all groomed to be, he became angry, and so did I. His anger was outward, mine was inward.

I didn't understand that this was all part of the competing inherent in growing up. I didn't realize that we were just trying to do our best in the face of two very accomplished adults who happened to be our parents.

None of us realized that our parents were struggling with the old and conventional while facing the new and unknown. As with any children, the four of us wanted to please our parents and the pressures to do this were often overwhelming.

And now I see families with grown children, especially those I grew up with. I watch them very closely, looking for the signs of the old family warmth unique to that particular family. Those things are so hard to find in this busy, modern changing world. Sophistication, secrets. It appears that so many of my old friends have changed and forgotten the value of their families.

Actually, I think the warmth of my friends is still there. It's just buried, overcoated by years of growing up in an ever-pressured world. A world that often makes us forget those things that are most important, like our feelings, our true essence which makes us special and unique. Love becomes an itchy, annoying, embarrassing word. We forget that our core is based upon our ability to show genuine love to friends, parents, siblings and children.

The love issue is so interconnected. This is what siblings often forget as they compete for the love of their parents often at each others' expense.

I'm lucky. Our parents never gave up on us. Even to this day, mom campaigns for greater family understanding. My brother and sisters have grown up to become wonderful and dedicated people. When my brother and I first encountered each other right after dad died, we hugged each other. It squeezed out years of unfamiliarity and signified the long but promising road of our friendship as adults.

My brother and I have so many similar goals. We were so bonded as brothers when we were young. Our lives are even more similar now; we're both in marketing, both working hard to provide for our families. But those layers of just plain growing up. We still have so much to peel away.

My relationships with my two sisters are very positive and loving and my brother and I are working hard to bend and understand each other better. We are doing what all adult brothers should be doing. Dad would not only be proud, he'd be breathing a sigh of relief.

Even when a parent dies, the healthy ideals never do. We all still try to make our Dad proud. He knew his sons would finally have the sense to begin a positive adult relationship with one another.

I guess all the parent can do is throw the football. It's up to the child not just to catch it, but also, to run in the right direction.

Sometimes you just have to settle for a field goal.

Because . . .

He was He.
We are We,

he was the best that he could be.

He was Then.
We are NOW.

He gave us love
and sweat of brow.

We had it all
yet nothing more

than hungry hands,
an opened door.

And Now to see what We can do.
The wife, the bills, the children too.

We face the old. We call it new.

Now is FOOTWEAR.
THEN was shoe.

7

SATURDAY-DADDYDAY

The Little Red Hammer

When I was little, when my little feet had no hope for touching the floor of our old '56 Ford Synthetic-Woody station wagon, dad would take me to a magic place some Saturday mornings.

Once inside this amazing place, as my neck craned upward, my heart raced. My eyes were as big as the lightbulbs on the rack or the paint cans on the far wall, stacked neatly to the ceiling.

This was the Chandler-Levy Hardware Store in Newton, Massachusetts and to my little soul, a hardware store meant that anything was possible. Daddy would take all kinds of shiny things from the shelves and some wood from the back lot. Then he'd hand the big man with glasses some green paper and silver things and off we'd go.

In a matter of hours, with the help, of course of my little red hammer, this collection of stuff would become a doghouse, or a new closet or even a whole new room.

Daddy, the hardware store, and my little red hammer. We could take scraps of stuff and make anything in the world. Those Saturday-

Daddydays were the happiest, most exciting days of my life.

Today, as a marketing person, my livelihood is based upon taking scraps of ideas and building them into marketable form. I've traded my little red hammer for a big white word-processor but it's funny. When developing a new campaign, if I get those same feelings I had in the hardware store, then I know the project will work.

Dad was a builder, a planner of great structures and so many other great things. His aim was to succeed and complete his tasks always in the best way he knew how. He achieved by circumventing nonsense and through the careful blending of wisdom and spirit.

And of course my little red hammer.

Sunspire

Standing at your grave
on a sunny Spring Saturday-Daddyday

waiting for your soul
to embrace my aching heart.

I relax
and drink up the loneliness,
aching to ignite
the spirit that was his spirit,
the soul that was his soul.

I rededicate my life.
I want to build something.

8

THE INSULT
SHADOW

The Insult Shadow

When my friend's father committed suicide fifteen years ago, my parents told me not to talk to him about it. There was such a sternness in their request that this one time, I didn't automatically do the opposite of what they requested of me.

Just last year, this same friend and I wound up skiing together for a day. There's something about a perfect ski-day, bleeding-blue sky, fresh air and all, that really makes you feel just great about everything.

We were adults and we could now talk about our fathers with freedom and perspective. On the ski-lift, I asked him about what he went through. I was struck by his clarity.

Faced with sudden immobility from a massive heart-attack, his father took an overdose of sleeping pills to accelerate the inevitable.

My friend spoke three simple words that really made me listen. "I was insulted," he said, explaining that he felt as if his needs and feelings didn't matter to a father who would escape his loved-ones through suicide.

Though my own father did not die from suicide, I experienced similar feelings. Especially for the first year after his death, I was insulted. How could he abandon me when I needed him the most? I was angry . . . Damn! I just met him.

The insult stubbornly shadowed me like an unrelenting arthritis. I asked, "Why, Why, Why!" though I knew no answer would make a difference.

As with my friend, I merely floated with this hurt and anger and watched helplessly as it solidified around me, wondering if it would ever dissipate.

I was not much fun that first year. Anger takes a lot of energy to carry around and it tends to spill onto the innocent who just happen to stray in your vicinity.

But the early winter finally abated and removed enough of the anger for me to be able to realize that one day, I would again know the joy of a contented skier.

So, now that some reasonable time has passed; To my mailman, my plumber and all those bewildered friends who strayed onto my property: That was not the dog, that was me under a shadow.

9

THE ULTIMATE
ORGANIZATION MAN

How Did He Do It?

There are many traits children inherit from their parents. While I feel privileged to possess some of my father's intelligence, drive, and spirit, I marvel at my own genetic aversion to order and organization.

Hard as I may try, that magazine and single sheet of paper I just placed on my desk have somehow multiplied into hundreds of papers scattered all about the room. It's nothing I did. It just happened.

On the other hand, there was my dad. I don't know how he did it or if the truth was that out of fear or respect or something, every paper clip just knew its place. He was that way with everything; each of his belongings was exactly where it should have been. Always.

For him, neatness was an automatic condition. It was this special sense of being able to organize anything. You could observe any aspect of this man's life and you would find everything clean and in its place. He was the overall organization man.

In the many buildings he engineered, he

personally monitored each phase of construction and would never tolerate any errors.

He was a man unswervingly ordered and principled and he expected that others were organized within their own realms. As amazing as the man was, nothing amazed me more than this brilliant sense of organization. We could always count on him to be well-grounded in his responses to us and to help clarify our thinking.

An organized man has very little confusion in his life. I ponder this as I look for a pair of shoes in the closet. I swear I put them right where they belonged and I even tied them together so they wouldn't get lost.

But somehow they found a way to magnetically repel each other and now they're both hiding somewhere in fear that I'll punish them once I find them.

So I sit here in my stocking feet happy for those traits that took while realizing that you can't have everything.

On Time

We all know punctual people. Those persnickety folks who seem to leave for their destinations at the proper time so as to arrive right on time, always.

One-half hour ahead of these folks was my father. He always left for appointments much earlier than he needed to and always arrived early. Even though he disdained waiting, he hated being late even more.

When leaving for ski vacations, we always left ahead of time. Dad would hurry us into the Station Wagon saying, "We're gonna be late." An hour ahead of everyone else and he was still telling us we were going to be late.

As I sat there wondering how we were going to be late, I saw a man so alive, so ahead of the clock, it was as if he felt seconds ticked away faster for him than the rest of us.

His consideration of other people's time was a gesture of great respect. As a result of all this "gonna be late" business, he had more meetings, did more business, knew more people and lived more life. To him the passing of time was the only power he couldn't control and he saw so much to do in this world.

When he died, I had the impression that he was just getting started and that his best times were yet to come.

And he would have arrived at those times one-half hour early.

Tunnel Vision

What is equality? Today it seems to be brought about by compunction instead of human nature. But my father taught me about equality many years ago before it came into style.

Being an ex-Marine and an honors Yale Graduate were not sufficient credentials for a good engineering job after World War II; not if you were also a Jew—hard to believe that was only 40-plus years ago.

In 1948, this gifted man took the only job he could get—as a "Sandhog." Deep in the frozen, unpressurized muddiness that is the underbelly of The Hudson was a young Gordon Bronson digging what was to become the Brooklyn Battery Tunnel. These were about the toughest working conditions a man could suffer through. Each man was treated with equal oppression under the sheer adversity of working deep in earth's insides. It was there he met some of the toughest; where he knew he was measured only by the job he did and nothing more, just like the others.

Digging, cutting, lungs fighting to aerate against the crushing pressure of this dark, hopeless underground. Dad didn't grow angry, he grew tougher, but not in the sense you might imagine. He grew tough against oppression and impossible odds. He worked his way out of the tunnel to become a lowly draftsperson for a small civil engineering company.

Working — building — working — building, nothing could stop this sandhog from climbing the ladder all the way to the top, and when he got there in the late 50's, he then became the "foreman" of his engineers. Even in the fifties, he hired from every race, creed and color. His concerns were an applicant's ability, enthusiasm and willingness to learn.

He always paid women of equal talent the same as their male counterparts, decades before it even became a public issue. There are hundreds of people who got their first big break in this world because Gordon was willing to see them as people first and foremost.

This policy of course extended to the handicapped, like the blind young man who typed letter-perfect from dictation.

Of all the buildings he ever built, his greatest project was the one he tore down—the walls that people place between each other. The tunnel had taught him well.

He knew there would be no light at the end of the tunnel unless he and his fellow men and women dug to it.

Fall Down Humor

If you ask most people what they felt made my dad so special, most would cite the characteristics of intelligence and courage. To me, his most superior attribute, his salvation, was his sense of humor.

It was a combination of my mom's philosophical insights and my dad's sense of humor that gave us the means to understand the issues of growing up. Most importantly, humor was our means to survive through the toughest times. More than a hundred times he had said to each of us: "A man without a sense of humor is like a wagon without springs, with each bump becoming a greater jolt."

He knew that humor could achieve the seemingly impossible task of exploding or dissolving anxiety. He taught that the power of humor could be the salvation at the end of impossible, the faint beacon at the end of excessive seriousness or reality, the promise that we could cope and find a way, that life would go on and we would eventually laugh at what hurt the most.

Sunday, October 5, 1974. 2:04 pm. I was photographing my older sister skiing on Saint Mary's Glacier in Idaho Springs, Colorado. The 60-foot rock and ice cliff I was overlooking was nothing new. I had been climbing and skiing glaciers my whole life and I was very sure-footed, even in ski boots.

Out of nowhere, a young hotshot whizzed by me, skiing at a show-off speed way beyond his ability. In a matter of seconds a little rut of snow swallowed him up and he was on his way over the side of the glacier, sliding about twenty feet and then bouncing onto the jagged rocks like a mannequin.

He didn't look very good from where I stood. He didn't look very good from where anyone stood but I was closest to him so I proceeded to hurry down the rock face to help him. At the highest point of this ledge was a natural area of rock steps that I could slowly climb down. Unfortunately, the first rock I stepped on gave way and I arrived at the bottom much quicker than I had planned.

The fall was over sixty feet. While falling, I knew there was no way to survive such a plunge onto the waiting rocks below. I said goodbye to the world and peacefully waited for the longest second of my life to pass into quick death.

The split-second finally ended as I put up my right arm at the last minute. The move had saved my life. I was elated, very badly mangled but elated. I had survived. My right arm was smashed, broken in eleven places, I would learn later. There were bones sticking out of my arm and blood was everywhere.

A week later I was flown back home to Boston for a couple of operations to save my arm. The evening of my arrival, my dad came to the hospital. There was plenty of concern on his face but his first reaction was this rugged, subtle breath of a laugh. "You really banged yourself up, son." I managed a little laugh myself. I survived something that should have killed me. I made it. There was more happiness than sorrow. The laugh signified that I had survived and would still be around.

Today I smile with relaxed confidence as I realize that dad taught me how to survive hard falls.

10

THIS DEMON
CALLED SUFFERING

This Demon Called Suffering

"Suffering was the only thing (that) made me feel I was alive." (From a song by Carly Simon)

I think of all those old Black & White films and those warm and loving country doctors. The family gathering around the dying patient's bed for that final goodbye, that final request from the heart to be honored by those who must carry on.

There's something very beautiful about a goodbye like that which must make the final rest all the more peaceful.

Today, the country doctor has faded away with the old movies. The new scene for many dying patients is that of living death, thanks to the miracles of modern technology. We postpone the inevitable and some guy out there must be making millions by selling the hospitals all those hundreds of miles of tubes which run in and out of these patients.

We are out to erradicate death and its companion, Demon Suffering. We have stopped thinking of life in terms of quality and only in terms of time, as physicians and courts around the world seem to battle for who kept the last human cell alive for the longest time. Billions of dollars are made by the simple premise that society not only wants to stay young forever but to live forever as well. We flock to seminars, schools and other dream places that promise systems for reducing suffering.

Nowadays, the worst disease of all seems not to be the one which causes death but death itself, and anyone connected with it. When dad died, no one knew what to say but the living still needed to be spoken to.

We were told by his doctor that he, "did not suffer", that he did not know what was happening and that his death was, "exactly like going to sleep."

We all breathed a sigh of relief as the doctor told us this a week after that horrible moment. To Gordon, it was just like going to sleep. When our household pets reach a certain age, we put them to sleep too and to the children of the world, there are millions of old dogs asleep somewhere.

My suffering was somewhat relieved as I learned that he didn't suffer, until a couple of years later when I discovered that this was a standard answer many physicians give when asked about the question of a victim's suffering in the final moments.

Why do we treat our old and dying like babies? To suffer is to endure, to tolerate, to make it through somehow. To learn, to grow and to love.

Suffering taught me that life isn't all good nor all bad and that if I can survive its lessons, I can live on and pursue a balanced life. Suffering, this great teacher of wisdom, lets go of its survivors and gives birth to opportunities for new joys.

Suffering isn't all bad. It's just another part of life we must learn to understand and live with. Should we bring back the old country doctor and those sacred last visits around the deathbed? The Hospice Organization provides a similar modern day version for the dying patient and that's a wonderful tribute to the real values of a family.

Even if it does involve a modicum of suffering for all parties, the saying of goodbye as a last experience seems a lot more sensible than turning off a switch.

Dad's death was so unexpected. No goodbyes, no warnings. I suffered after he died. There's a little place of loneliness that forever stays with me for him and that suffering helps preserve a sacred memory and a basis of my strength.

There's a much bigger place in my heart for my own children, new and excited about this world and their expectations from their daddy.

My adversity has made me wiser.

11

THE LUXURY OF 'WHY'

"Lite" Puppy

I guess death is about as final as things can get in this world. It's the only thing that can't be undone. And life just relentlessly marches on.

A baby's best buddy, her poor old dog, can sustain life no longer and dies. The baby doesn't really understand, she just wants her doggie back. As a parent, you'll do anything to stop those big eyes from getting bigger and more tear-filled. A few days later, the little one is presented with a brand new puppy. In minutes the smile returns; the old dog, forgotten.

My brother very sensitively explained to his three-year old how things began and then ended. "You go to school, you come home again."

Then he told her, "Papa's life is over."

Though she loved grampa very much, she did not cry. She did ask if her other grandfather would still be around and was assured that the rest of life would be as it always was. There, of course was no capacity for deep lamentation, no asking, "why?".

For us, the question of why bounced back and forth in our skulls with ever increasing momentum. Finding out how he died could be answered but why did it have to happen to him? That's the unanswerable question that you keep asking in a world devoid of the luxury to answer.

The why's bounced furiously inside my head until about five days after his death when I encountered my wife's grandmother, whose intelligence and grace add youth and beauty to her ninety years.

Though it was difficult to see anyone who was enjoying a longer life than my dad's, I trusted her wisdom and looked to her for some saving words. She took my hands firmly, gave me a hug and said, "I'm sorry dear but that's the way it goes."

And that was all she said about it. No great lamentations, no lectures, no cheerleading. In this age of lite bread and beer, here was a lite phrase that worked. At that moment, I just stopped asking why because I understood. There was no changing, there was simply coping.

Too many times, dad used to say, "You can't always control what happens to you but you can control to a great extent, how you deal with it."

Sure would be nice to hear him say that just one more time.

That's the way it goes.

12

THE TECHNOLOGY HE'LL NEVER KNOW

For His Sake

Now and then, I'm haunted by this scene that seems born from one of those old Bogart movies. A thick white mist opaques all but an image of my father standing on some railroad tracks. He's not waving, just standing there in one of his fine suits. His eyes, neither angry nor peaceful, are frozen directly on me.

I'm standing at the back of a caboose of a long train. I cannot take my eyes off him nor can I keep the old rickety train from steaming away. He grows more faint in the distance as I extend an outstretched arm straining to reach him. I know he can no longer come along. He stands there solidly, watching me.

Every few months this image comes to me, usually triggered by a new technological development or a major news event, or merely something I put together that I just have to tell him about. Often it hurts to see life steam on and leave him transfixed in history.

He had incredible wisdom about the latest business and political situations around the world. His uncanny sense of logic and comprehension caused many around the world to seek his wisdom. I was often overwhelmed, feeling defeated before I ever started. Maybe that's why his stare is still so strong even as time moves on. He was so dedicated to building his wisdom, we never imagined ever having to pull away without him.

I hate to see life churning on full steam without him, not just for the sake of my mother or the rest of us, but for his sake. He worked so hard to enrich his life in every way, he should still be part of it all.

Did something go wrong just this once? Maybe the Gods meant to take another person. Why take a man of such value so soon? Where does it leave us?

Stop the train! Go Back! For his sake.

13

RESPECT

The Expectation Curse

Dad was a tough, tough act to follow for anyone who knew or worked with him but no one can know as deep a sense of burden as the child of an accomplished parent. Others who knew him could aspire and set their own limits. His children are driven by the fact that the potential for success is in their blood.

Respect is not an inherited condition, although many children seem to get respect because of who their parents are. As the son of my father, my very existence felt good. Living under the protective shadow of this man, I enjoyed life in the shade. I believed in myself no matter what because my father was strong and he believed in me.

Society looks at the son of a respected man with a certain scorn. Being a child of Gordon Bronson seemed to mean for some the automatic gift of unearned luxury and the best opportunities to be the best. But in truth, nothing came free to us.

The reality was an excessive drive either to remain level-headed or to spend the rest of life wondering why the world didn't instantly appreciate the child of this great man.

Dad's death was tough on each of us for many different reasons but I know I was the one to most quickly get used to his physical absence. That's only because I lived in California for the five years prior to his death. I was already well on my way towards discovering how little I knew. Love, business, marriage, with no parents by my side to watch every move, life was testing me and I was flunking badly.

Failing really scorched my soul, paralyzed me until I observed that messing up was how life tests and teaches us. I probably could have remained close to the nest and ended up with a very comfortable life, as did many of my peers. But I was part of the have-it-all, live-forever pre-yuppie set. For me, having it all was trying to get it all on my own. I taught myself to be brave and confident, no matter what. Eventually, I learned to learn from my mistakes and not dwell on them. I understood the beginnings of respect—self-respect.

When a beloved parent dies suddenly, your foundation crumbles. All geography aside, now you're really on your own. Life gets glaringly real. Then people watch you and judge you, people that you never had anything to do with. These are the friends of your parents who watch to see if you really have the stuff to pull your life together and these are the people from whom you seek respect.

Seeking this respect can really haunt you until you get smart enough not to care about it. Although a death can seem to force you to grow up and clean up a lot of psychological garbage, it induces illusions of maturity. Death can accelerate reality but not necessarily maturity.

My dad and I respected each other because we loved and believed in each other. To attempt to fill that void would be a foolish waste of time. I work hard to maintain the respect of the people I love and that's it.

Dad made no specific demands of our lives except by his own example. If he asked anything of us, it was that we strive to become the best we could be in sculpting our own lives. If he did any pushing at all, it was to push us out of the shade. He was a tough act to follow but a great one to lead from.

Permission

So much of what we ever do is based upon permission be it blatant or subconscious. Very simple. As youngsters, we do or do not because a parent or other authority figure tells us so.

As we grow up, we test our boundaries of permission, often stretching them to discover or indulge ourselves. Is "adult" the label we achieve when we learn to give ourselves permission? Adult places, adult behavior, adult movies?

As strong an example as he was, dad did not deal with issues of permission, preferring that we learn by consequence. He was very relaxed that way. He saw the world as a reasonable place that would permit rewards for those who earned them. And he earned them.

The pressure and frustration of trying to win the approval of our father overwhelmed us. With all he did, and all the liberalism we enjoyed, we never really felt we had permission to fail, until the lawsuit took it all away. After years of a legal battle to hold his interest in the business he built up, he lost it all.

I'll never forget the day we gathered to hear the news. My dad was not the father I had known. He had lost everything and nothing we said seemed to comfort him.

So we all went back to our jobs. I recall feeling great pain for his loss but at the same time, feeling selfishly free. For the first time, I saw this great and powerful man as one of the rest of us, as human.

Immediately, I felt as if a great weight had been lifted from me and I could attack my career without fear of failure. I finally had permission to fail.

Oh, he had always said, "I don't care how many times you fall flat on your face as long as you get up and try again." I never believed him. He was such a model of success. I kept picturing all of us with very flat faces.

After the suit and startover time, I found I loved him even more. He became more open about his feelings during his financial convalescence. For the first time, he talked openly about everything and we developed a quality adult friendship.

I grew to see life as a series of triumphs and failures and that it was okay. I saw his real value as who he was to his loved ones. And he was magnificent.

As time passes,
I get up,
and I fall.
I get up and I fall.
Each time, I grow closer to humanity,
flat face and all.

The Platitude Puzzle

I always took great comfort in platitudes, you know, those few correctly ordered words that seem to explain a disproportionately larger concept. You can spend weeks, months, years agonizing about something until you encounter that perfect sentence.

"Aha!" you say. "I get it now. That explains it." Then you strut around in perfect psychological comfort, the crisis solved forever with just a few magical words.

When dad was in one of his platitude moods, he had a tendency to hide an otherwise warm and brilliant personality. He had platitudes for everything. You could bring up a subject and he'd knock you flat with a platitude.

When a conversation grew stale, he would switch to "Platimatic."

"Dad, should I get my boss's approval for this new plan or should I just go ahead and try it?"

"It's Better To Ask For Forgiveness Than It Is To Ask For Permission," he'd respond.

(Uh, oh, the Platitude Trap, what do I do now!) "Well Dad, I don't know . . ."

"What are you afraid of?," he'd assert.

(Hey, that wasn't a platitude. I broke through!) "What if it doesn't work," I'd ask, expecting a real reaction.

"If You Fail To Participate In The Events of Your Time, You Run The Risk Of Never Existing At All."

(He's switched to Platimatic. What am I gonna do?) "Come On, Dad. I can't joke around with this," I plead.

"A Man Without A Sense Of Humor Is Like A Wagon Without Springs, With Each Bump Becoming A Greater Jolt."

When he wanted, he could recycle a select few of these same proverbs to fit almost any conversation. He could be a real show-stopper. Or he could just be real.

He delivered those sayings like old jokes and we collected them as if they were essential pieces of a giant puzzle that, once assembled, would induce a universal chorus of billions of screaming souls shouting, "I get it."

I could go on but like he said, "After All Is Said And Done, There's A Lot More Said Than Done."

"Oh, I get it."

14

"We Interrupt This Life . . ."

What Would He Say About Us Today

As funerals go, dad's was what you'd call a good send-off. Truly an impassioned eulogy, the Rabbi spoke with as much love and wisdom as words could convey.

The burial, such a final goodbye, hurt like nothing ever hurt in this great universe. As the limousine headed home from the cemetery, I focused on the world outside. It was a crisp fall Sunday. Dad would be outside raking leaves.

Back at the apartment, I felt as if I were walking within a different dimension from all the people there. I was waiting for dad to walk up to me, put his hand on my shoulder and say, "Don't worry about me. I'm dead but I'm okay. Now you get on with your life and make me proud."

Life is so different without him. We never would have moved back East. I'm sure we would have waited much longer to start a family. And I would have simply settled into my staid advertising career.

Instead I find myself as part of the nest I left fifteen years ago. As siblings we have tried to be fathers to each other, and mother occasionally recalls what she feels would have been his appropriate wisdom for the various challenges that we have faced since his death.

Our failures at this activity only cause us to miss him more and also makes us realize how special and rare the man was. He left no instructions, and even if he had, the void is there and it cannot be filled.

I miss discussing world politics with him. I miss his praise when I made him proud. I miss his impatience when I made him angry. I know if he were watching me today, he would be annoyed at how much time I think about him, and how much power he had in my life.

I can almost hear that warm, deep, assertively clear voice saying, "Enough about me, my time is over. The greatest thing you can do for me now is to put my death behind you and move forward with full determination. Anything else will be a waste of your time and of my effort in raising you to be a solid human being."

"Great, dad, that's easy for you to say. You're dead." His words are so faint without him standing here facing me. He always looked me right in the eyes, and the words marched from his soul to mine.

As you try to honor the words and wishes of a dead parent, you wrestle with this new self you have been discovering since your life was so rudely interrupted. You had to become a new person to adjust and survive. You became your own boss and new bosses take on bigger responsibilities, make bigger mistakes and realize greater rewards.

Life offers such bizarre trade-offs.

The Resting Place

Parent's are powerful figures to most kids. Growing up, I never knew how to behave in front of these completed humans. They were different from us. They were a different form. We weren't going to grow up to become adults one day, were we?

Here we were as kids bouncing all over the place, never seeming to rest, full of perpetual fun until some parent pointed a finger and said, "Stop the fun. Do something unfun, like taking out the garbage or walking your sister to school."
And school! That was another one. Parents sent you off to school, only to be bossed around by other adults. To top it off, mother was also a teacher. She was one of them and she was one of those.

Being a little kid was a time of doing without ever knowing why, while slowly discovering that these parent-forms were not only being parents, they were making money and feeding us. Wow! As if we weren't already overwhelmed.

In time, most kids grow up, have their own children, and discover why their parents were always pointing the finger at them. They see their parents as other adults and not as some overwhelming source of brilliance that seem to know everything.

That never happened with my folks. They both seemed to grow wiser as I grew older. Mom remained the parent/teacher and I discovered that dad was a truly brilliant source of information, not just for us but also for his friends and business associates.

Seeking his wisdom became a habit. Dad's intelligence gave him the correct viewpoint more often than not, and me, a place to rest my questions.

Much of his knowledge came as a result of years of study, discipline and a dedication to excellence before "excellence" became the hip thing to strive for.

Since his death, I study like I never did before—I think with more completeness while hoping with all hope that at least some wisdom can be genetically inherited. I am driven by a man who reached beyond the stars.

As if I weren't already overwhelmed.

The Last Wet Postcard

(Slapping-drenching rain today, that furious early spring kind that renders outdoors into nothing more than a wet postcard.)

Alone in my car, I am struck by an intense feeling of cozy security. Rain like this is my insulated break from a rushing world. I take a deep breath, relax and think at a warm and comfortable pace. I can stop the world and take a good look, unless I think of my dad's last rainy day of life.

Mom and dad were having a relaxing dinner with my wife's folks. Dad's leg was in a full cast. Ten days earlier, he had undergone a procedure known as an osteotomy, which essentially was a reangling of a lower leg bone in order to allow for more movement of the knee.

Dad was an avid athlete and the surgeon had strongly recommended this procedure as the most logical means to continue an athletic lifestyle. "Don't worry, son," he had said, "this is a pretty straight-forward procedure. I'm just going to be laid up for a while. That's all."

So ten days later, during that relaxed dinner when dad said he felt a little light-headed, no one thought much of it when he excused himself from the table and hobbled into the den.

Then came that eerie sound.

It was a strange enough groan to have frozen the table conversation. They hurried into the den to find him slumped back in the chair, his eyes rolled back in his head. Within a minute, he snapped out of it. "What happened!," he said.

He was sweating uncontrollably. His breathing was labored. An ambulance was called. "I need oxygen," he demanded of one of the paramedics.

"Hold yeh horses, I'm working as fast as I can," the medic replied. Within minutes, dad was wheeled into the ambulance, speaking no other words. It was raining much like it is today.

Sometime in the ambulance, amidst the piercing yell of the siren in the rain, he was last aware of anything. Alone, fading, dead. Was he scared, angry, depressed? At peace? Did he know that these were his final moments?

I want to know but I will never know.

Had it not rained today, I might never have included this story. I tried so hard not to write this one. It's a hard story with hard, cold concepts, too hard for someone you love.

The Death of a Great Mind

I had heard the story of his final moments so many times, my brain had to react with a dream, a terribly vivid dream. My subconscious could have called it a nightmare and switched it off but my curiosity won over.

In my dream, I became him at that final instant. Only at that last fraction of a second did I know my life was over. My body was already gone. Panic. This is it. No turning back.

The rush that all I knew to be life, rising and swirling, a cacaphony of 60 years of blurry noise, every sound I ever knew, hurled outward in one final uncontrolled roar.

The swirl of noise—fading, fading until an unfamiliar voice, an old soft voice moaned, "Life goes by so fast." The swirling noise spiraled ever more faintly into forever.

You don't know . . .

what I went through.

You can't say

I had no right
to mourn my way.

You can only pretend
until it happens to you.

Is He Still Around?

Two days after his death in the middle of an extremely still night, the oddest sensation jolted me out of a sound sleep. Someone had just "walked" through me, as a ghost would. It was my dad and it felt so comfortable, so natural, that my only reaction was to peacefully drift off to sleep again.

That morning I woke up thinking about that strange experience. It wasn't a dream. It was an occurrence of some sort. I said nothing about it to anyone. I didn't want to find myself written up in the Enquirer.

That morning, mom told about having almost the exact same experience. She described him moving around in the air. She believed that he was still around in some form.

Others reported similar experiences. Rational people talking about irrational goings on. Even me. Being the type who always sought logical explanations, I reasoned that these events were simply post-traumatic reactions, viz. the natural behavior of our psyche's comfort mechanism. We experienced these things because we needed to believe somehow, that he was still around.

Aside from the warmth of family and friends, those first weeks of discussions were loaded with stories of Gordon dropping in or I should say "floating by." Everyone was seeing signs. A coin or two found in a significant place, dream visions, feelings. To top it off, a psychic friend of my mother and younger sister appeared, or maybe I should say, visited us a couple of times. She told us that Dad was content and dancing for joy in his pre-transition to the "other world." As dad was never much on dancing, I had my doubts.

I politely smiled each time she gave us these updates on Gordon's new life. Since this lady was psychic, she was probably reading my mind and realizing how artificial my smile was.

As the realities of life confronted us in the weeks that followed, the visions all disappeared. The psychic told us that it was because Gordon had finally made his full transition into the other world. What do I know about it all? Well, if he were there in any form, he would make his presence known. He was always one to make his presence clearly known.

Then again, he always told us that, for something to be real, "you had to believe in it." So I'm torn. My logic tells me not to believe in an afterlife, but then maybe if I believed hard enough, as my father always advised, I might find that he was with me all along.

The truth is we don't know for sure one way or the other. We are left with this battle between what is real and what we think is real. And maybe something else. Maybe some outer force does guide us and my dad is trapped in that medium, screaming *"Why don't you answer me!"*

I don't know, Dad. Maybe it has something to do with the breakup of AT&T.

15

GOODBYE DAD, I LOVE YOU

Argument For One

It's a lot easier to make peace with your parents before they die.

"You're gonna drive your poor mother to the grave." Most of us have heard that one in a somewhat comedic setting. The parent holds him or herself hostage in a usually vain attempt to produce a certain behavior in a child.

Then one day, it really happens, the thing that we never talk about nor want to know about, the thing that could never happen to our parents. Their life ends either from illness, old age, or from an accident, as with my father.

Even death from old age is often completely unexpected and hits the children as a complete shock. Death of a parent is usually the only thing that proves to a child that their parents aren't immortal.

A parent's death certainly doesn't automatically resolve and/or forgive any conflicts. For the surviving child, major unsettled parental disputes can remain frozen in a perpetual argument for one.

When I received that fateful phone-call, my dad and I had no major conflicts. The last three words I had said to this man the night before, were "I love you," not because I feared anything was about to happen, that's just how we always ended our conversations. As fate would have it, that was our final goodbye and it was a good one.

But what really matters is not the last words but the tenor of the overall relationship. He loved all of us, powerfully and in different ways. And now, as several years have passed since his death, I think we all realize that we had a good friendship with our father. It was the quality of the long stretch versus a moment of mere words at the end of a phone call.

In California, one of my bosses was a self-centered father of two grown children whose greatest panic was that his hair was greying. This very accomplished man pulled me aside one day and asked if I would clandestinely buy him some hair coloring so he could hide those bits of grey that were beginning to appear on his head.

My father was very meticulous about his appearance but he would never dream of hiding his greying hair. As his children, we knew we gave him most of it and he wasn't about to hide that fact. At age 60, his grey hair was the only real evidence of his age. He was in very good shape.

The grey hair was proof that he wasn't going to live forever, no matter what our illusions were about parental immortality. It was a message we all heeded as we sought to shape our parent-child relationships into their respective adult phases.

As an adult, I understood that my dad was a crucial force in my life. It finally dawned on me that my mother and father wanted to love and help me in the best way they knew how.

Though I was committed to making it on my own, I found much greater joy in life by sharing my business adventures and misadventures with my dad. In his last couple of years, whether bestowing business or personal advice, he was coldly direct, telling me what I needed to hear versus what I wanted to hear. He knew what my aims were and he was gracious enough to share his wisdom. His was the only advice I really believed at the time.

For many, the prospect of making peace with parents promises to be the toughest fight of their lives. If however, you begin today, right now, to attempt some inroads, you'll be glad that you at least made the effort.

Learn to appreciate the value of your parents before they die and you will create a peace that will help guide you long after they're gone. Even if they are now gone, you can still resolve your differences and make peace with your parents. Let them rest in peace and then you will live in peace.

Old Files

Page by page,
days pile up
like old files in the corner.

Do not fear each year
as bringing you closer to death

But welcome the turning of the pages
as bringing you richer in wisdom.

The Babies He'll Never Know

What is it we live for, why are we here? For me, aside from all my lofty career ambitions to better this world, my major focus is to love and nurture my children, my babies. Sometimes all the rest seems like fluff.

I suppose this is based upon my innate need to see life go on, to perpetuate the species. To show a wrinkly brand new little baby to an excited grandmother for the first time is a moment of deep pride and great solidarity.

With this great and pure joy there was a painful sorrow, for it was a moment robbed from my father. He knew my brother's beautiful girl in her first joyous years but will never know the rest of the generation he has grandfathered.

Shortly after dad died, my brother talked about how much of dad lived on in his daughter. With two of my own little girls now, I certainly understand what he means. I can see my father. I can really see him, in their little eyes and their little hearts.

He lives in these children so vividly and when life is at its most rational and most peaceful, I hug my babies and suddenly life flows between us with a serene joy greater than life or death. My children are my ultimate promise to this world and to my father.

No matter what happens to us in this world, including our own death, our children are the promise that our most essential selves will live on.

My lessons of this continuum came so much earlier than I ever dreamed. Perhaps this rude acceleration compelled me to look at it all with an intesified perspective. And the sparkle in my babies' eyes teaches me things that I never would have otherwise cared about.

He'll never knew these babies but they will know him.

Smiling Moon

Golden Star,
Golden Star
I Look At You
You've Come So Far
Twinkle Face,
Magic Girl,
Sleeping in
a magic world.
Let your dreams
not fall apart.
Let me stay
inside your heart
Twinkle Face . . .
        . . . Golden Star

Life Prayer

I walked into the Sharper Image Store recently to buy myself a toy (for completing this book, as a matter of fact). I was wondering what my dad might think about all these new gadgets when it happened: I heard player-piano music. It seemed oddly out of place in this high-tech store but it was there, automatically playing the old favorites, using new tech to awaken old memories.

The moment the keys began their charming plink, I was nearly overwhelmed by a sense of tearful sentimentality. (If I did cry, I'm sure the Sharper Image would have had some kind of high-tech Kleenex for me to use.)

It was his song and I hadn't heard it since he had hummed it. For years, no matter the occasion, and as tone-deaf as he was, dad would hum this tune. "Da de da da da da de da de dum." We could be skiing in a blinding snowstorm and I could always locate him by that faint "da de da da da da de da de dum." Yup, that's dad.

He wasn't much for lyrics or tune, so for many years, I didn't know what that song was. In fact, for most of those years, I didn't know it was actually a real song.

Then one day about a year before he died, on a Saturday-Daddyday, we were building some new stairs for our Cape Cod house. He started in with his "da de da de."

I finally got up the nerve to ask him, "Dad, what the heck are those de da's? Are you singing, are you practicing new ways to talk to children, or what?"

"You don't know that song?" he responded with surprise.

"Well . . . , not quite like you hum it," I said meekly.

He explained that it was the "Young Lovers" tune from *The King and I*.

Of course! After all those years, I had cracked the code. "Da de da da da da de da de dum" was actually: "Hello, young lovers, whoever you are . . .

I hope your troubles are few
All my good wishes go with you tonight
I've been in love like you.

Be brave young lovers
and follow your star
Be brave and faithful and true.
Cling very close to each other tonight,
I've been in love like you.

I know how it feels
to have wings on your heels
and to fly down a street in a trance.

You fly down a street
on a chance that you'll meet
And you'll meet
not really by chance.

Don't cry young lovers
whatever you do.
Don't cry because I'm alone.
All of my memories are happy tonight
I've had a love of my own."

Loving Strangers

Today was supposed to be a research day. I was one of those people at the Boston Public Library, buried under a mountain of books, arduously pouring through poetry, psychology, statistics.

I wanted to know my audience a little better. Sure, I had talked to numerous subjects before I began and of course, wherever you disagree with my philosophies, I am hiding behind poetic license.

As I dug through item after item, ad infinitum, Shakespeare took on new meaning and provided great comfort. Now that it wasn't homework, I drank in MacBeth and King John with an insatiable thirst.

One of the last pieces I went through stopped my machinery, closed down my brain. It was an Institute of Medicine study entitled, "Bereavement: Reactions, Consequences and Care." The numbers: Over 800,000 spouses die each year, almost half-a-million children die. In total, over eight million Americans die each year, most from perfectly nice families like yours and mine.

"Wow, book, you mean at least 1 out of every 36 people I see each day is mourning the loss of someone."

"Possibly."

Here I've written this whole thing on my personal anguish as if I were all alone. In the meantime, at least eight million people were probably going through something similar. At least eight million. But I was alone, wasn't I? And if I was alone, what makes my ordeal so special? Why my story?

I climbed out of the stack of books and shuffled out of there. What was I writing about! What right did I have and what help could my writings possibly be?

Outside it was a snowy, hopelessly bitter cold late afternoon. Despite what my dad had taught me about resiliency, the icy chill enveloped me as if I were wearing no clothes at all.

As I drove to the Cape, heater on full blast, I approached the exit that lead to the cemetery and swirved onto it at the last moment. Dead or alive, dad had to answer some questions right then and there. I still had so many questions!

As I approached the cemetery, the snow reflected just a glimmer of light from the blackening, blowing skies. The faint howl of the dancing winds sounded like a dying whisper as I located the section where he was buried. There are no stones at this cemetery, only bronze plaques over the burial places.

I got out of the car and trudged through the snow to his grave. Under a couple of inches of new snow was the iced-over kind and my feet broke through it.

All the plaques were partly or totally covered but even in the dark and snow, I knew his spot. I stood over the grave, waiting for something to happen. Sometimes, my visits were tearful, occasionally I'd talk to him and kind of give him a general update, the world as I saw it in news-capsule form. When I was sufficiently relaxed, the place became a growing spot.

But this time, I stood there and nothing happened. I was just too anxious. I drew in a deep breath and slowed down my thinking as I told him I'd find a way to work this out. As I cleared off his plaque, I made an interesting discovery; I was not at his gravesite.

I laughed. I really laughed as I thought of how I had just poured my heart out to a stranger or I should say, the memory of a stranger. I was laughing securely like dad and I used to do together but this time I was exploding the anxiety myself.

Suddenly thoughts were racing clearly again. The laughter must have shaken it loose. I ran to the car and scratched out some notes on a napkin before those thoughts could scatter away in the aimless, windy snow.

I still have that napkin crumpled and sitting in my desk. On it are scribbled these three simple words: "We bury pain." I arrived home that night and wrote furiously into the morning, the words flowing painfully and insecurely.

This writing had a purpose again; To help people unearth the pain and not just to bury it away somewhere as a confused mental blur. We have to look at this painful time over a long stretch and accept and deal with it as we grow and not just hide it away.

A decent burial can take years. So why my father, why not something about your dad or your mother, spouse, sibling or friend? This *is* for your loved-ones. As I realized when talking to the stranger at the cemetery, there are many issues of love, life and death that are indeed universal. And if we share our pain instead of burying it, we will heal.

This is very personal stuff and it has been a scary and difficult experience to write it down. But since this writing, life has become new and exciting again. I celebrate my children who gleefully welcome the newness of life every day.

And I am the father now.

So I speak to you and your loved ones so that my pain may be your strength.

Dear reader,

We sincerely hope that this book has been helpful to you in some small way. Both Bestsell Publications and Mr. Bronson are grateful for your many kind letters and we appreciate the many reorders for family and friends.

To express our appreciation, we have developed a generous discount schedule for reorders:

Quantity	Cost	Shipping	Total
One Book	$8.	$2.	$10.
Two Books	$15.	$3.	$18.
Three Books	$20.	$3.	$23.
Four Books	$22.50	$4.	$26.50
Five Books	$25.00	$5.	$30.
Six to Ten Books	$4.50 ea.	.65 per book	
Eleven to Fifty Books	$4.00 ea.	.35 per book	

Please send check or money-order and quantity requested to:

Bestsell Publications
c/o Bronson
6 Samba Circle
Sandwich, MA 02563